Express Yourself!

 By Tiny Toes

Illustrations by Harper Meadows

Happy

Can you show me your brightest smile? Let's light up the room!

Your smile makes me so happy. It's wonderful to see you smile!

Silly

Silly, funny face! Let's make silly faces together!

It's okay to be goofy. Laughter makes us happy!

Angry

Uh'oh, someone looks mad!
Can you show your mad face?
Everyone gets mad sometimes.
Let's find a way to calm down together.

Laughing

Giggle and wiggle, let's laugh together! Laughter is the best sound. It means you're having fun and being you!

Yawning

Aww, you look so sleepy. Let's get you comfy and cozy.

Sleep helps you grow big and strong. Sweet dreams, little one.

Sad

Sad eyes, my dear? Let's cuddle close, I'm always near!

It's okay to feel sad sometimes. We can always find a way to feel better together.

Kissing

Kisses for you and kisses for me! Kisses make us feel happy.

Shy

Peek-a-boo, I see you, my little one.

It's OK to be shy, we're here with you.

Sleeping

Look at you, my sleepyhead, resting so peacefully. Sleep brings new adventures for tomorrow.

Grumpy

Uh'oh, someone is feeling grumpy! Can you make a little grumpy frown?

Everyone feels grumpy now and then. Let's hug and feel better.

Dirty

Uh'oh, someone needs a bath after all that play!

Getting dirty is part of the fun! We'll clean up together.

Surprised

Look at you, so wide-eyed and full of wonder!

Being surprised is part of the fun of discovering new things!

Thank you so much for making it this far!

I'm truly thankful for the time you dedicated to reading my book.
As an independent publisher, your support is invaluable, and I sincerely hope your children find joy in it! 😊

If you could spare a minute, your honest review on Amazon would be incredibly meaningful to me. Your feedback not only greatly benefits the book but also allows me to learn from your experience with it!

How to leave your feedback

1. Activate your phone's camera
2. Aim your mobile device at the QR code
3. The review page will appear in your web browser

Thank you!

Made in the USA
Coppell, TX
12 September 2024

37149669R00017